Ice On A Bench

Richard Jennings

Table of Contents

A Thing You Should Know Before Reading This

So before your read what I've written

The poems about life, love, and being smitten,

Losing sleep and going mad,

Being torn and feeling sad,

I feel like you should know something about this work.

Putting some of these words to paper seriously hurt.

There were some that I didn't know if I should write.

They were too honest and I didn't think it would be right.

But a good artist holds nothing back when he creates.

Even when he can't finish all that's on his plate.

So I had to do it really. I had no other choice.

This is the deepest work I have ever given voice.

All Bark and No Bite

People do a lot of talking lately but talk is cheap unless you back it up

So unless you're going to follow through, close your mouth and keep it shut

Because I'm tired of picking up all the slack

Things people say they'll give when they lack

Paying off other's debts is not my job of choice

So don't make promises you can't keep and you won't have to pay with your voice

Even when you're only talking about money the rules are the same

Don't bet at the tables if you can't afford to lose the game

Because money's always going to talk,

But it's not worth a thing if it's all that you've got

Because money's only power if you're using it right

And I can tell you're not because you're too afraid to bite

The dog that only barks is the one that gets bitten

And it gets even worse when he can't pay the deal that he's stricken

So back up your money, back up your mouth

Or you'll end up with your face a little farther down south

Now pull your head out of your ass kid and listen to this

You back what you say, or it's your own ass you'll kiss

Consequences of a Shallow Decision

You're a suicide pack strapped to my back

The chemistry between us is the powder you lack

I'm running full throttle and I'm not turning back

The world's about to crack and I'm happy for that

So I'm jack smacking a mac in the back with a bat

You got a cat jacked cause wanted to chat

Now let me tell a cat he's about to get jacked

So listen up Jack before my vision is black

You may have been smart but you were lacking at that

Ran your mouth and now you're laying slack with a bat

Don't run away you better get back and attack

Or I'm a put this baby bunny back in the hat

Better Lies

I'm afraid

Every day

You can see it in my eyes

When I say

I'm okay

Because I've told you better lies

And it's not

What I want

When I'm telling you goodbye

I want you to

Look me in the eyes

And tell me that I lied

Ask Around

Let me be real with you, and stop the facade for a moment

Let me show you who I am so I can finally own it

I'm not a king or a saint, that's all just an image

I'm benching that personality and everything with it

But I'll keep spitting bars in my personal hell

Rearrange them to look like a prison cell

My rhymes are lame and pretty predictable

But picture this and let me paint you a visual

Imagine walking uphill in the rain with a boulder

You've got the whole world and its weight on your shoulders

It's getting harder to breathe as you're getting older

And the closer to the top you get it keeps getting colder

So by the time you reach the peak your body is lifeless

Now imagine every single day is just like this

I'm not trying to impress you or ask for sympathy

I'm giving you a tour and letting you into me

But don't get that twisted either this isn't depression

Well what is it? And that's a great question

I would tell you but I don't rightly know

It's just my job to come and give you a show

I could pick apart almost anything else

But I run out of words when I'm explaining myself

So don't trust me when I try to tell you who I am

Anybody else would do a better job than I can

Wether I'm smooth or awkward, cool or a clown

You'll only find out if you ask around

It's hard to know me when I don't know myself

It's easier to talk about somebody else

But messages get twisted up in poisonous words

So you can ask around but forget what you heard

Bleeding Love

You surround yourself with poisonous people to kill the
emotion
Because you gave up on the one who promised love and
devotion
And now that you've made your bed to lay in it's rockin'
like an ocean
And as you reminisce you find you're sick of going through
the motions
So you bury the regret of losing what you needed
Because you were too busy telling yourself you didn't need
it
But now when you try to sleep your brain finds every way
to repeat it
And the memories cut your heart so deep you can't help but
to bleed it

Broken and Bitter

You know, I would have gladly taken an apology. But then you went and gave my heart a lobotomy, and now I'm not how I ought to be, because you fucked me up like sodomy. So don't think I'm okay with these games anymore. Don't act like this duck is a lame anymore. Because things just aren't the same anymore, and I'm not waiting for you to change anymore!

Games are for the pieces and the players

People are puzzles with lots of layers

And bullets may go through vests

But arrows go through chests

Broken hearts are a girl's favorite toy

But the bitter ones belong to the boys

This is my list of terms and conditions. If you agree, I better not catch you switching positions, or I'll drown the whole world in a pile of munitions! I'll rip the heads off of all of these bitches! But forgive me, I tend to lose control. I tend to say I'll do things that I won't. And I try to believe that myself but I don't. Because I really will if I don't get what I want!

Games are for the pieces and the players

People are puzzles with lots of layers

And bullets may go through vests

But arrows go through chests

Broken hearts are a girl's favorite toy

But the bitter ones belong to the boys

Pride and Shame

If we went to war and you had to pick your side, the pride of the shame, or the shame of the pride, would the proud be ashamed that the shamed don't lie? Would the shame of the pride bring shame to the pride? Would the pride be ashamed of the shame of the pride? Would the shame of the pride be ashamed of the pride? Because once we're shamed, we're all the same. And many have died, for less than pride. So if we went to war and you had to pick your side, how proud would you be to be ashamed of your pride? Or would you be too proud of the shame to be ashamed of the pride? So if we went to war and you had to pick your side, would you pick the pride of the shame or the shame of the pride?

City Dreams

I can see the city all around
And I feel like I could drown
In all the buildings and the faces
That I found in this town
From thirty two to three hundred
South to Broadway what of it?
The buses are packed
From the front to the back seats
People on the corners standing
Waiting for taxis
Shadows in the alley
Waiting for drug deals
People spending money
Just to see how the rush feels
For some reason
It seems like nobody can drive
But when you're walking in the city
What a time to be alive
Because the city ain't as bad as it seems
Everybody here is just chasing their dreams
When the sun goes down
And the lights come on
They go to catch their dreams
And tell the city so long
But I can look down broadway as far as it goes
Thinking about the things that nobody knows
It's just another question that needs to be answered
How do I dream when my sleep has been canceled

It's simple enough if you can get what I mean
Because I don't need to sleep in my city of dreams

Communication (Two Way Street)

I hate when people ask "why don't you text me?"
Because communication is a two way street
You make no effort to include me in your life
What makes you think I want you in mine?
Not deserving the title of friend
But expect me to be there in the end
And I will, I always will
And not for the thrill
But for your own benefit
Because I don't want either of us to regret it
If I'm not there when you need me the most
The hero, the savior of the lost
My heart is larger than I can handle
But don't put me on a mantle
I'll pick you up when you're down
I'm your lifeguard when you drown
But I've learned not to expect the same
Because I needed you and you never came
So when you ask why I don't text
I want you to think of it as a test
And maybe then you will see
I don't want friends who don't deserve me

Cleaning a Mess

It's hard to imagine all the pain that I cause

When someone only mentions my name and you pray to
God

And I can't begin to fathom how we got so lost

Last I checked you were stuck on all the things that I'm not

But we've moved on and this is something I guess

That can turn out in the end to really be for the best

And even though you took your clutter I'm still a mess

You were the only reason I had to care so what did I
expect?

Soon enough I got sick and caught a case of cabin fever

I had to move my mess or decide on where to leave it

So I put it on your door step and I walked away

Little did I know you went and threw it away

I guess looking back it's kind of easy to see

You did the same to my mess that you did to me

I should have seen it coming but I was partially blind

So blind I didn't see you going when you left me behind

You left me with my mess just us two alone

And you left me with the keys to abandoned home

You let me keep the car that I couldn't drive

Because it's hard not to crash when it's hard to survive

Your love was the reason that I stayed alive

But when you left you left me highly deprived

But I've learned a lesson as I've gotten older

I've learned to clean my own mess and I've gotten colder

So when you see me next time and you give me a wave

Look back at when you left me and the mess that you made

Look into my eyes and realize it's finally gone

Somewhere out there I finally found it a home

Some broken hearted girl has something to tell you

In the remnants of the mess I gave her she can still smell
you

But it's organized and clean and all packed away neatly

She found a way to fill up all the holes and complete me

I would introduce you to her but I'm not sure

You might be okay with that but I don't know about her

She might make me choose which of you that I hold nearer

But the answer couldn't be clearer if you looked in a mirror

You're really not the same girl you were when you left

You realized that I'm not the only one with a mess

So you came back into my life and said you needed a friend

I gave you a place in my heart that was reserved for a guest

When we spoke things awoke that were hidden and dormant

We got back together, we said forever, we were both still important

So even when you're down and feel like nothing is true

Just remember that forever means I'll never stop loving you

This was the story of what could be the future

If you'll only clean the mess and fix up the loser

Consolation Prize

It's nice to finally see where I stand. A great last option for a backup man. A consolation prize for a runner up. Not even the crime but the cover up. You would rather aim for less, than think and settle for the best. And when the best isn't your goal, you've dug yourself a hole. All they want to do is get in it. I've only been trying to get you out. I'm a prize and I wanted you to win it. But all you ever did was doubt. So close your eyes and say a prayer to the constellations, because I'm a prize but I won't be your consolation.

Cry to God

I've picked my poison to kill the monsters in my head. But here they lie, with me in my bed. I can't seem to figure out where I went wrong. And in the future this was a memory all along. It's hard to see what's wrong when nothing's ever right. And since my thoughts are always dark it's getting harder to see the light. I keep drowning in my sorrows, it's a story I'll never tell. And no matter how damaged I get, it's a soul I'll never sell. I seem strong because I won't let you see me cry. And when my tear drops fall I hope they end up in the sky. Each tear to me is a prayer, Angels watch me as I weep. So I'll send God a message, tears before I sleep. And I've got a lot to say, so I hope he likes to read. Because I need him to come and find me, I'm lost and feeling weak.

Cracks in the Sidewalk

I've never been known as a liar and a cheat

But when I write it's from the heart, to the rythm of the street

If I listen close I can hear the city's beat

In the horns of all the cars and the shuffle of our feet

The way the rain is falling all along the concrete

There's too many people for me to ever meet

And too many faces that I could never greet

But if I work hard I'll be the one they want to see

As it is now they only barely shuffle past

Everyone is rushing but nobody's going fast

No one shows up first but ever wants to be the last

So they shuffle on moving as a mass

I'm not a part of the crowd because of how I walk

Headphones in, spitting rhymes when I want

But nobody ever listens when I talk

They just keep staring at the cracks in the sidewalk

Cut Off (Road Closed)

Go ahead, cut me off
If you don't want me
It won't be much of a loss
Yeah, you'll see
Close the road between you and me
Destroy everything that we could be
It's not like I trusted you
Not like I cared about you too
But that was all sarcastic
The measures you took were drastic
Go ahead and cut me off
It won't be much of a loss
To lose someone who doesn't want me there
Won't be a reason to gray my hair
It's no skin off my back
If you don't want me watching yours
It's not like when we talked
That I would let my heart pour
You knew a lot of pieces of me
And all that I could be
I didn't know enough about you
To know what you could do
So go ahead, burn the bridge
Don't look back at what you did
I won't, I'm walking away
To chase a brighter day

Devil's Due

Playing games with strangers is a dangerous game

The Devil could be playing with a different name

The game and the rules are all yours to choose

But it doesn't matter because he doesn't lose

And every dollar lost is a year you'll never get

But you'll never know so go ahead and place a bet

You may just be invincible in the life ever after

But losing to The Devil might end your current chapter

He'll lie and he'll cheat so you'll never have a chance

Cover your cards but you can't escape his cheating glance

You claim the kingdom four times over and get up to go

But he'll drop his hand with just as many aces in the hole

You pray to God but he already cashed out and left

So your consolation prize is a trip to the depths

Dream Work

The clock strikes four and it's deep in the morning

I'm still awake because just dreaming is boring

Why would I waste time imagining what I want

When I can write lines with the talent that I flaunt

I'm never satisfied with where I am in life

I always want more of the struggle and the strife

Hunger is a part of me and how I've been raised

So working towards my goal is how I spend my days

I'm not afraid of overtime in fact I volunteer

Every time I'm on the grind I'm smiling ear to ear

Poems and songs, lines and bars, I write them all

I write all day and every night. I'm waiting for a call

The phone will ring and they'll tell me to take a break

I finally made it now and fame is mine to take

But I'll talk back. I have something to say too

Breaks are for the satisfied and I've got something to prove

I'm hungry, and that's the way I stay

I don't talk shit I just spit my game

If it's sunny or covered in rain

One day fame is going to walk my way

Downhill

I look up at the mess about to spill
And remember that it rolls downhill
It's how I see things nowadays
When negativity seems to be the will of fate
And people keep telling me to keep my head up
They say it can only get better
But I've caught enough to fill a cup
And my jacket's only getting wetter
Because I'm at the bottom and I'm trying
And whoever said this was easy was lying
Climbing up feels good but it doesn't last long
Another wave comes to prove your footing wrong
So you slip, and tumble, and fall head over heels
And again you remember how the bottom feels
and one more time you try to climb higher than before
And you do the best that you can to reach for more
But how many times can you get back up?
How long do you have before you get stuck?
Eventually there's going to be too much to deal with
And you'll accomplish nothing but drowning in it
But I'm smart, and I know what I'm doing
Because even when it's taller than me I keep going
Because there's a secret way to win
The thicker it gets, the easier it is to swim
So I'll use the downfalls for my own gain
And I'll reach the top through the rain

Drown Out

I play it loud
I scream it louder
And when I'm up
I'm on some downers
My heaphones broke
I'll bump the speakers
Can't drown my thoughts
Hand me a litre

My music's so loud that I sing when I talk
And it's still not enough to drown out my thoughts
But if I use it, I could be more than I'm not
And if you'll give it a listen I'll give it all that I've got
My music's so loud that my ears are always ringing
I can't hear the world over the sound of the singing
Honestly I don't know what the hell I was thinking
Shit I can't remember what the hell I was drinking
My music's got me up but my drink has got me down
I'm thinking straight in circles and I'm spinning all around
In my current state people think that I'm a clown
But they must be mistaken 'cause the circus ain't in town
I'm just a sad man sadly surrounded by pain
I've got vultures for thoughts just surrounding my brain
And the music comes down like the sound of the rain
I've got some inner demons that I can not contain, so

I play it loud
I scream it louder
And when I'm up
I'm on some downers
My headphones broke
I'll bump the speakers
Can't drown my thoughts
Hand me a litre

It's 4 am again on yet another sleepless night
I swear I've tried it all just to set my demons right
Never in my life have I put up such a fight
When I stare into the music, that's when they can see the
light
As the volume grows I slip and fall into a trance
The demons lose their shit and they all begin to dance
They're so distracted that they give me one more chance
They can't tie my shoes together and they can't pull down
my pants
No longer will I suffer from the torment I endure
I slip away and lock the door without another word
Then the sound of breaking glass is all they ever heard
Fill the room with alchohal, light it, watch it burn
Fill the sky with smoke, sit back and watch it bleed
Giving me all the satisfaction that I'll ever need
With the demons gone angels come and they can breed
Maybe they can straighten out the life that I lead

I play it loud
I scream it louder
And when I'm up
I'm on some downers
My headphones broke
I'll bump the speakers
Can't drown my thoughts
Hand me a litre

Erasers

When you're writing with a pencil and it scrapes

You can turn it around and erase your mistakes

But you can't erase the mistakes of your past

The bad memories stand out because the good never last

But if you try hard enough you can dull the roar

Fill the page with doodles until you can't see the words

They won't be truly gone, you can see them if you try

But even if you do you'll only ever wonder why

Because the memories that hurt aren't easy on the eyes

But making ones that don't can cover up the lies

So when you look back at where your pencil slipped

Don't try the eraser, keep on using the tip

The Story of I

Sometimes I feel like I have no home. When even in a crowd of people I feel alone. Surrounded by people, my so called friends. But I feel by myself all alone in the end. It's not something I can help, no cure. It's a curse placed by a world on the ignored. But I no longer feel the pains of remorse. Only the regrets of a man through divorce. Though I've never been married, but to a dream. And that dream I fear will be the end of me. So as I bid my last adue, I tell the story of myself to you. Sadly saying so, this is the end. But the beginning of the tale is just ahead. Who I am is dying and will never be the same, even though remaining are my face and my name. So let me tell you the story of I, and how it came to be that he died.

Drunken Father

Breathe the darkness, ride the high

Never stop to wonder why

How or who or where you are

What you did outside the bar

When you fall no one's around

So turn your face and kiss the ground

The concrete rubbing on your stubble

You fell face first into a puddle

There's a smell you just can't miss

As you lie there in the mist

Sirens coming down the street

You'll never get back on your feet

You can't run or even walk

You can't even think to talk

It's not your fault you lost your job

It's not your fault you're just a slob

You can't be blamed for being mad

But you can be for being a horrible dad

Instead of your kids you picked the booze

You couldn't win so you chose to lose

That was years ago, it feels like today

When they came and took it all away

But now you've got your shit together

You've been on the wagon what seems like forever

You've got your son and his little sister

You couldn't tell how much you missed her

Your little girl and her older brother

Both of them look like their mother

That's the thought that gets you thinking

That that was the thought that got you drinking

But you won't ever be that man again

You've found a new beginning in the end

Every Morning

Wake up and flip the switch to check the power

Grab a towel, get undressed, and take a shower

Dry off and shave just to feel a little fresh

Even if my face really isn't a mess

Throw on some clothes and deodorant too

Think about the things that I need to do

Breakfast is quick if I even eat

Shove my shoes onto my feet

Grab my bag and head on my way

Into the morning to face the day

Fear No Evil

I'll throw a hand in the air to signify the charge. Living someone else's nightmare but I'm living it large. I'm one step ahead of the game. Playing against a villian without a name. Some say he's not that bad at heart. Some say his heart is empty and dark. But I fear no evil. There is no chance of losing this fight, because I've never been wrong, and the winner is always right.

Fire in the Furnace

I'm about to head home and get a cup with some ice in it.

Hit the room, pop a bottle, and try to feel right with it.

Drinking is all I seem to be good at these days.

Drinking is the only thing that kills the pain.

It doesn't even matter if I'm under age.

I drop the bottle back and feel the fires blaze.

My insides burn and boil and it hurts so good.

There's nothing quite as soothing as a bottle to the blood.

After a meal if my stomache needs help to burn it,

There's nothing like whiskey to put a fire in the furnace.

It keeps me warm in the winter, and hot in the cold.

It may be bad for my body, but it's good for the soul.

Whiskey, Vodka, Beer, and Rum.

I don't feel right until it's all gone.

Wines and spirits, dark and clear.

Bring that bottle back over here.

I've had enough when I say so, not when you think.

So keep your grubby hands the hell off of my drink.

Plastic cups or bottles of glass.

Throwing it all up in the grass.

Shit-faced, hammered, plastered, smacked.

Sauced, wavy, seeing black.

Out with friends, or at someone's home.

I'm going to drink until the drinks are gone.

They Tried To Hold Me Back

They tried to hold me down

To keep me on the ground

They tried to hold me back

To make sure my plate was stacked

They thought I couldn't handle the weight

That I would give in to their choice of fate

They tied me up and left me dying

But I never gave up on trying

That's why you heard the story I told

Revenge is a dish that's best served cold

From Day One

From day one I had this dream

My eyes have always had this gleam

And as simple as it seems

I say exactly what I mean

And I don't mean to have it all

I just mean to have a ball

Order pizza, make a call

And maybe start a brawl

What's life without some fun?

What's love without the one?

Why do we give all for none?

And where's the corny pun?

Because this isn't fun

I don't think ever was

Will be or is, because

I'm working from day one

Trying to go from here to done

And even if I was one the run

Every day would be day one

Generation Out of Touch

It's a sad situation when your entire generation lacks the
motivation to chase the separation of receiving the
sensation of a standing ovation from the rest of the nation.
When you receive compensation even in the inflation it's
outraging when the hating stops the celebrating. It's
penetrating our minds, and leaving us blind. And if you'll
look then you'll find that all you're leaving behind is a joke
to laugh in the face of time.

He Doesn't Remember

Forget your boyfriend, forget what your mama told you.
Acting like he really cares, pretending that he really knows
you. I bet he doesn't know half of what I know. All the
things you feel and you don't show. Like what words really
hold in your heart. What the names of your future children
are. But I do, and I always will. I'll never forget the nights
we let our hearts spill. It's a gift, and a bit of a curse,
because you'll always be the one that I want the worst.

Gravity

Look me in the eyes and anchor my soul to the ground

I'm going to let you be my gravity and hold me down

Because I lost my mind somewhere up in the clouds

And my body is following your lead as we dance around

You have this affect on me every time we're near

I would fly away if you weren't the one swaying here

Guide my body with yours, it's impossible for me to steer

Don't let me fall down, just let me hold you so dear

I'm running laps in my head on a track on could nine

You've got me lifted and it happens every time

I took off around when you said this dance was mine

I can't think straight enough for my usual corny lines

I'm going to keep my eyes on you and let you be my gravity

If I start to day dream please don't get mad at me

I can't top this when you're the best of my reality

Hold me down as I start to lose my sanity

Wrap your arms around me nice and tight

Keep me from floating away to the light

You're the reason why so it's only right

Be my gravity and hold me down tonight

"He's Different"

Yeah, sure, he's different

Did he tell you that himself?

Do you expect me to believe it?

Because I don't, oh well

You said that about the last one

And the one before that too

And every single one of them

Has said the same about you

So if they were all different

How did they all end the same?

Tell me, what's the difference

When they all end in pain?

You should try something truly different

And just stop all together

Take some time to yourself

And you'll finally do better

Because as it is now

You're not getting very far

All these guys really want

Is your bare ass in their car

So do yourself a favor

And for your own sake

Do something different and stop dating fakes

I'll Be Back

I feel like it's time for me to go. Put the key in the car and get ready to roll. Head down south or maybe out west. See if home really is the best. Because I feel like I've got to keep moving on. And I know I'll miss you when I'm gone. But it won't be long until I come back. There's no doubt about that. I could never stay gone for too long. Because where you are is where I call home. Home is where the heart is, way back where it started.

Hookup

This girl was an angel I can't tell you why

But whatever it was it was deep in her eyes

The brightest of blues that could wash away lies

Immediately I was hypnotized

She had me shook all it took

Was a look I was hooked

Locked up and booked

My goose had been cooked

Like a bell I fell

Into hell where I dwell

Every time I'm forced to tell

The tale of the tail

That left me on bail

I would sail through snow and hail

To bring her mail with sand in a pail

That piles on pounds

Surrounded by sounds

All around

Of people that drowned

From town

And now I found

That I'm going down

In the sea

That I see

And I can't believe

I can see

It was me

I was deceived

By the light in the sight

When she lit up the night

I would fight any plight

To set my life right

Because she was not what I thought

The thought that I caught

When I bought her a shot

Blame the pot she was hot

It's your fault

It's not

I just needed something to believe in

But what I believed was an angel was really a demon

And now it's too late, I filled her with semen

And sex before marriage has made me a heathen

I Am The Fire

Feed the fire, set me off. Watch me explode like a molotov.

Ever growing, always stronger. I only dream of burning longer.

Run and yell, scream and shout. But you can't seem to put me out.

I AM THE FIRE. I BREATHE. I BURN.

I AM THE FIRE. NOW WAIT YOUR TURN.

I destroy, I consume. Everything I touch I use.

I crackle, I crush. And everything I take is too much.

But I come and I take it anyway. You can only watch it fade.

I AM THE FIRE. YOU SMOKE MY BREATH.

I AM THE FIRE. YOU KNOW YOU'RE NEXT.

How I Started

Let me tell you something about how I got involved in poetry

When I was young, there was nothing anybody could show to me

I thought I knew everything I needed to know in life

But then a girl ripped my heart out with my own knife

So I had to cope somehow and I eventually found a way

Life can be hard when you have a lot to say

Especially when you don't know how to put it to words

But paper always keeps a secret when it burns

That's basically how I got started

And learned to fill the hole where my heart is

But eventually there was something people needed to hear

It was a message I needed to make a little more clear

So I wrote it down in a hundred different ways

And I published a book in a matter of days

So now that I made public how I cope with the things that I deal with

People understand my messages more because they can feel it

How to Act
They try to tell me how to act

But I always keep it clean

They try to tell me to toughen up

But I won't treat a lady mean

I'm the type of guy

To take my heart and spill it

Chivalry's only dead

If you're the one who killed it

Never take it back

When I say the magic words

And I'm going to let you in

On a lesson that I've learned

This is how to act, and it's never been a secret

Take the best you've ever been and find a way to beat it

Treat everybody right, until they prove it wrong

And even then don't get revenge, that's why karma comes along

It never hurts to give a dollar to the needy

So try to give as much as get and try not to be greedy

Try not to think negative and don't ever forget

These lessons are to keep you from living with regret

How To Break My Heart

Start it off with the most crippling blow

Start me soft and build me up real slow

It's the painful torture that gets me hooked

The small things like your smile as soon as you realize I looked

And the way you say my name when you want my attention

Make me want you so badly it stops all thoughts of prevention

I'll give myself up willingly and lower my defences

I'll blind myself completely and tear down my own fences

So when you step it up I won't even see it coming

Clear to everybody else but I'll never know I should be running

That's when I'll plug my ears to everyone but you

Ignoring even myself if it's what you want me to do

And when I'm at my worst convince me it's my best

Run me ragged and never let me get any rest

Eventually you're going to have to bring me down

Do it easy so I see myself begin to drown

Make me watch myself fall apart over the very idea of your loss

Then finally walk away and show my feeble heart that you were always the boss

I Remember

I'd ask if you remember, but I know you don't. Every word
I said, every word I wrote. But I do, I can tell you that for
sure. I even remember the words you never heard. I'm sure
you knew what I was saying, but you never truly knew
what they meant. Every time I said them I kept on praying,
that they would get to your heart through your head. You
used to say it back but now you don't. I'm not sure if it's
because you can't or you won't. I take it as an answer to
my question. And it serves as a reminder of my lesson.
That's why I remember the words we used to say. And
that's why I remember way back to the day. The day when
we chose them. The day they were spoken. The day that we
fell, and how easy it was to tell. I would give a lot for a few
more days like those. But only you can decide the way the
story goes. The climax to our story is still impending, and
only you can control the ending.

If I Were Indestructable

Let's say I was indestructable, and couldn't feel any pain

I would probably go recklessly drag racing in the rain

I would get in a gun fight like nobody could stop me

I would step in the street and take on the entire town posse

I would jump off of the tallest building I could find

I would find a mountain and begin to climb

With no harness or safety nets to save me if I fall

I would fight wild animals big and small

I would go to the White House and sit in the president's chair

I would find a shitty celebrity and set fire to their hair

I would go to war and win it all by myself

I wouldn't even have a partner to ask for any help

I would do whatever I wanted because why the hell not?

I would start with swimming in lava just because I like it hot

I wouldn't have to worry about girls leaving marks

I could challenge every dog that wanted to bark

I could hug a cactus and piss on the third rail

I could resist arrest and break myself out of jail

I could go sky diving with no parachute

But if this was you what would you do?

In The Fallout

Maybe we can find love in the fallout of this mess we've been making. We can play it like a scene on this set we're creating. Maybe when they clear up all the smoke, and all that needed speaking's been spoke. Maybe they'll find us living happily ever after, in the wake of their eternal disasters.

I'm Solid

Anger on my mind and a freezing cold shoulder. These memories couldn't move me, I'm more solid than a boulder. She wouldn't let me hold her, felt like I mind body and sold her, so she told me it was over. But I never broke when she said it. Though I never thought she would dead it. I kept myself to my own and I never did regret it, because your past can only haunt you if you let it. Do you get it?

That's what it's about. This is why I'm loud.

I can be a rebel; this is why I'm allowed.

Because I'm built like a soldier,

And I'm only growing colder

Every day I'm getting older.

It's a tragedy, but why don't you try

And help instead of getting mad at me?

I'm Going to Grow a Garden

I'm going to grow a garden, full of plants so green

That all the animals will gather and lay under my tree

The song birds will whistle such a sweet, slow melody

Yeah I'm going to grow a garden, a garden just for me

I'm going to grow a garden, and you are not invited

I'm going to be there all alone, living deep inside it

My garden is going to be way too big for me to try and hide it

But that idea is just too absurd for me to even try it

Because I'm going to grow a garden, and sit in the shadowy places

Why would I ever want to leave, and see the world of shadowy faces?

Because outside of my garden, everybody's going through the paces

Yeah, outside of my garden, are men with suits and brief cases

I'm going to grow a garden, because the rest of the world is grey

I'm going to stay in my garden, because it's the best place I can stay

I won't come out of my garden, and there's nothing you can say

Because I've been growing my garden, since the day you walked away

I'm going to grow a garden, of all the things we couldn't be

I'm going to fill my garden, with all the things you couldn't see

I'm going to feed my garden, with tears for every tree

Because you left me in my garden, just my garden and me

Impossible Heroes

Impossible heroes are impossible not to believe in

There to stop the lies and deceiving

With all the qualities of fearless leading

Always a quote to part with when leaving

An impossible hero is what children want to be

They want to be the greatest person they see

Every child inside including me

Wants to make dream into reality

From Robin Hood to Superman

Batman and Robin with lethal hands

Doing everything they can

To be the best kind of man

The inspiration to be what we want

To have the ability but not to flaunt

The impossibilities of a hero are a dream

But the possibilities are endless with a team

Intentions

If your heart aches I've got a cure, but it's hardly conventional. And my intentions may not be pure but they're purely intentional. So let me listen to your troubles, come here, tell me what's wrong. I'll tell you what you need to hear and maybe sing you a song. I'll make you forget your worries, and everything that ever hurt. All it takes is a bit of time, and hiking up that skirt. Because medicine isn't cheap, and forgetting isn't easy. Take it from experience, the winds of love are breezy. So let me help you help yourself and we can get it done. And all you're going to have to do is come and get it on.

It's not about how wrong it is, it's more about how right. It only takes a little while, maybe even just a night. Forget about that other guy and all those stupid fights. I'm the one in front of you promising to see the light. This can help you, this I swear, I'd never lie to you. That could just be a lie, but it could still be true. I could tell you anything, you'll probably want some proof. But all that I have is my word, so what am I to do?

You don't need to thank me, you don't owe me a thing. But I want you to remember, you can give my phone a ring. I'll always be here for you, this isn't just a fling. That may be some other guys, but that's just not my thing. I won't leave you helpless, because I really care. Or else I wouldn't even bother playing with your hair. And if I'm lying it would show, I wouldn't meet your stare. But it's my word to God above, and on my life I swear.

If your heart aches I've got a cure but it's hardly conventional. And my intentions may not be pure but they're purely intentional. So let me love you like I'm supposed to, love you like I should. Let me love you the way only someone who really loves you could. You can forget about those other guys and all the stupid fights. Forget about all that was ever wrong, I'm here to set it right. There's a lot of things I'm good at, but only one I love to do. Because of all the things I love the most, I favor loving you.

Lost and Alone

When you're lost on your road, look to your side. I'll be your hand to hold, a ride or die. I'm feeling bold, and kind of sly, but truth be told, and I won't lie, I'm down for you, if it means a fight. Nothing I won't do, to set things right. I promise you the time of your life, if you'll just call me tonight.

Just a Friend

Yeah, your girl's a friend of mine

We call it a love thing

One of those "she's thinking of me,

When you put her above" things

And I know she liked the way I spat when I spit

Because she got my lyrics in a tat on her tit

So imagine how long

She's going to be with you

Pretty soon it's "so long"

And she'll be leaving you

And she'll be calling me to come and pick her up

While you're home alone and feeling down on your luck

But I wouldn't worry about your relationship's end

I mean after all, she said I'm just a friend

Keep it Simple Stupid

My name is Richard Jennings and I've been deployed
And I'm not allowed to leave until this page is destroyed
When I write, my main mode is intelligence
And if you don't care, then that there is irrelevance
Sometimes, I get a little carried away
And if you don't mind, I might get a little married today
See what I mean? I'm a mess
But that's the first sign of being a genius
And there I go again calling myself the best
Is it too much to ask for this that and the rest?
I always take on more than what's good for my health
I guess my eyes are just bigger than everything else

I should remember
Someone should tell me
Just keep it simple
Don't go and get crazy
But that's just not how I roll

My name is King Richard I like to exaggerate
If you don't get it yet then let me elaborate
Sometimes I talk like I'm somebody else
That's because my brain ran away with itself
I don't really have limits, I don't like to hold back
But sometimes I forget to reel in the slack

It's a slight problem I can't seem to manage

And it's not the kind of thing I can fix with a bandage

But I wouldn't know because I haven't tried

I kind of enjoy being out of my mind

As long as I don't end up confused

Because I don't like to mix pop with the blues

I'm bantering again, I'm really very sorry

Going off topic is a kind of hobby

When I'm ruling the world I can teach you

But until then I have things to do

Make it Rough

Put me up against the wall with my hands behind my back
and frisk me.
Tell me how talking back can always be used against me.
Read me my rights and tell me what you're going to do.
Don't be afraid to leave a bruise and maybe a scratch or
two.
Because we like it rough that's how we roll,
And when we love there's no control,
Because we can't contain this animal.
So cuff me up and let me go.

Knight in Dirty Armor

If your knight's in shining armor I've got news for your
king
Because his knight has never had to fight for a thing
So before you give your hand
Search across the land
And with the blessings of your father
Find a knight in dirty armor

I'm a knight in dirty armor
I fight for my beliefs
I don't get all the glamor
Other knights get to see

Now I never was a showboat, the spotlight was never mine

I was always in the background, but every man has got his time
And now the battle's over I remember why I fight
To marry who I love, as is everybody's right
So take my hand and don't be afraid
I'll face every challenge in our way
Nothing they could do could ever hurt me
Because I'm not afraid of getting my armor dirty

If your knights in shining armor I've got news for your king
Because his knight has never had to fight for a thing
So before you give your hand
search across the land
And with the blessings of your father
Find a knight in dirty armor

I'm a knight in dirty armor
I fight for my beliefs
I don't get all the glamor
Other knights get to see
But if you'll do me the honor
You can come with me
I'll show you what dirty armor
Can really come to mean

L.A. Cap

I wear an LA cap because I played little league
Tried to do things to make my dad proud of me

59

Tried to be a person he'd be proud I could be
Because he passed away when I was only 14
Left a boy alone to face puberty
And try growing up in a world so mean
At least I can say that I know that he loved me
And I'll swear up and down to the God above me
That I'm doing what I can to try and live my life right
And if you can hear me dad don't let me out of your eye sight
Because I want my kids' kids to have a better life
And the journey to the future for me starts tonight
So when the road gets dark daddy send me a light
And when I close my eyes give me a kiss goodnight
I'll see you again when I finish my fight
And with a bit of your help I could make it out alright

Like My Status

Surfing on the internet, social media websites

It's getting late, and inching closer to midnight

I'm a little hungry, other than that I'm alright

But in my head, my heart is putting up a hard fight

I'm surprised you liked my status about the love I can't show

But I honestly wonder what it is you think you know

Because there's nobody special I've fallen for recently

There's nobody head over heels just dying to be with me

When you like my status like that I don't know what to do

Especially since a status like that can only be about you

You're the one I post about when I wish I could make you mine

But liking my status isn't what I meant when I asked for a sign

I wish you would send a sign that really matters

But go ahead, nonchalantly like my status

Liquid Faith

Few beers back, it's nothing but a feeling. The way she makes me feel, it ain't nothin but I'm kneeling. Now I know that I'm no saint, everyone's a sinner. But everytime she smiles, I feel like I'm a winner. Now it might be the beer, 'cause I'm not thinking what I'm saying. But I wish she was mine, until then I'll keep on praying. Beer gets me thinkin' 'bout her quicker. But there's not a lot that's stronger than the liquor. Either way I drink 'til dawn, and I don't know what's going on. But I wouldn't trade a day to say the words I pray would make her stay. I just pray she'll make the choice on her own. That she'll be with me when I'm grown. I have faith and I could never doubt her. Because this alchohal makes me think about her. She's not even mine yet because I get too nervous. I wonder how she would feel if she heard this? Would she agree that it's a good idea? Could that lead to us at Ikea? Would she turn the other direction? Could it be I'm not her type of selection? But like I said I have faith in the fate. I just hope it's not too late.

Listen to Our Song

I was waiting for the last song
But I waited far too long
You never came to dance with me
Never took the chance with me

I'm standing here alone
In the rain outside your home
I'm playing our song
On the radio I brought along

But you won't come to hear
The song I once sang in your ear
You won't even come to see
The band I paid to come with me

They pick up tools of their trade
The instruments they start to play
And they play our song out loud
I'm hoping you can figure it out

I did all this to show you
But there's so much I couldn't do
And I wanted you to know
So I'm showing you I love you with a show so

Hear these words
Open your window
See the boy
You pretended you didnt know
Give me the chance
I've been waiting for
So come and dance
I won't wait anymore

Options

Yeah that's right I got options. Got women set to hop in.
Venues I could rock in, and things I could be copping. I
don't need what you got, but I can get what you want, and it
wouldn't be a thought, I could wear it just to flaunt. I
believe they call it stunting, when you're out and copping
something just to show it off for nothing because the haters

tongues are running. I call it compensation of the over variety. And Greed is a demon that you'll never find inside of me.

You're a person, and a bad one too. And I got a lot of needs but they don't include, self-centered, greedy, sons of bitches like you. That's not the kind of person that I want in my crew. Because I can never tell what you're going to do, and I get the struggle but I'm not trying to get screwed. So I'm glad I could find people better than you. People that are here for me tried and true, and want to help with what I do, and I can help them out too, to fill the table with some food. Then we can all have options, and the freedom to choose.

Love and Murder

So sick of hearing what you're not saying. So tired of the games I think you're playing. Things we've said but never heard. Because actions speak louder than words. I love you deeply. But do you want to keep me? I will never let you go. But first I need to know. Do you love me? Or are you just saying what you think I want to hear? Do you love me? Or are you just trying to keep me here? Oh so near. To you my dear. To you. Shall I give you my heart again sweetie? Shall I hand you my universe neatly? Shall I devote every moment in time and every bit of my existence in space? To you my dear. To you. Maybe I should write it in the sky. Rearrange the stars to show you why. Three words I've said a thousand times. But you answer with what I fear may be lies. So tell me now, and God help us both. Tell me the truth, and may it not be dull. I need to know. Before I go any further. You have to choose between love and murder. Before I progress with the life I call mine. Have I properly invested my time? Because I love you. There is no other way to say it. I need you. I have no other way to explain it. Swift answer begets something swift to come about. But first I need the words to come out of your mouth. There isn't much time before I lose my mind. I just need proof that your words aren't lies. So tell me not with the word of tongue. But prove through actions that you weren't a liar when you were young. Kiss me and let me feel your passion. Blood will boil and emotions amassing. Kiss me and let me feel your soul. Kiss me and let me know, or let me go. Before we go any further. You've got to choose between love, and murder.

Money

Get that green, spend it fast

Nothing's cheap and that shit don't last

If you're like me with a regular job

You work just to pay for a few days off

Money comes and money goes

Where it goes, no one knows

Cars and clothes, food and hoes

Buying toys and watching shows

But that's just the way that real shit rolls

And South is the way that shit just goes

But it's all good, buy some shoes

Find some shirts and cop those too

And hope there's enough to pay your dues

Because if not I'd hate to be you

But sometimes it sucks to be me dude

Because people can be awful rude

To someone who thinks the way I do

Like I deserve way more than you

And I should be rich before I'm through

But I guess that that shit just won't do

Because I've got a lot to prove

And if I fall then I'll see you soon

Money is the motivation

Happiness the destination

That I'm preaching to the congregation

Across this forsaken nation

Go on twitter and get your follows up

I'll go on tour and get my dollars up

It's not fair and I know it sucks

But I put in work, this wasn't luck

Because money is a cruel game

You get your 15 of fame

But as soon as you get lame

You lose every penny to your name

So keep it simple and live it easy

The ways of money can be so breezy

But there's no need to go get sleazy

To get your bread a little cheesy

My Ocean

I'm sorry I wasn't your idea of perfect

I'm sorry you didn't feel like it was worth it

I'm sorry that I didn't pull the world apart when you tore
mine in two

But I'm mostly sorry that I wasn't good enough for you

But I want you to know that I grew up and changed

It was impossible not to when I was drowning in pain

But nowadays I'm swimming in it like a private pool

And chilling on a couch raft laughing like a fool

I've been busy living and I've forgotten the water beneath me

But even a wave or a storm could never beach me

I've gone too far out and I'm lost at sea

Lost somewhere out there in what couldn't be

But I don't need a hero, I don't want to be rescued

I'd rather rock with the waves and dream of being with you

I'd rather swim in my sadness than swallow my tears

It's made me stronger than all of my fears

So if you find yourself sailing or see me floating by

Come a little closer float on over and say hi

But if you're in my ocean there's a hidden meaning my friend

And if you're here, you should know I'm willing to try again

Because loneliness is cool but not if it lasts forever

I enjoy my ocean, but I'll swim to shore if we do it together

Puppeteer

The world is in your eyes as you stare at it, while it's dangling from the ends of your fingertips.

You watch as the world does silly things, as you sit back and laugh, pulling the strings.

My Type of Chick

If you want me to, then I'll be down for you

But don't ever forget what that really means

I'll be down to play, and I'll be down to stay

But you better remember to be down for me

I'm talking about my type of chick

A ride or die type of chick

An I wont lie type of chick

That's down for my type of shit

She's got to be fun

And she's got to have class

With a beautiful smile

And a pretty nice ass

She has to love to laugh

With a sense of humor to boot

So whenever she laughs

I can laugh too

She's got to be strong

I'll need her to hold me down

Keep me steady

When I'm stumbling around

She'll need to understand

I'm a little bit complicated

And if I ever find her

I'll be glad that I waited

That's what I want in a girl

That's a girl I could be with

I would search all around the world

For a girl I'd like to be seen with

Nerves

Calm down

Breathe

Focus

Think

You're shaking

Panicking

Clammy

Weak

You've got to fight

Play

Try

Compete

Don't worry

Relax

Plan

You'll be great

Keep it together

Push

Win

Relief

Never Enough Time
In Loving Memory

It always hurts to lose a friend

You never expect it to be the end

All the time in the world is never enough

And whenever you're alone it's like a punch in the gut

It's like a sunrise on a rainy day

It may get nicer but it'll never go away

You sit and think and you can pray

But there's nothing you could really say

It's not a physical pain you can take medication for

And it's like a hunger you can learn to ignore

It's a hurt down in your soul that rocks you to the core

And you know nothing will be the same anymore

It hurts even more when you swallow the pain

So you try to hide by crying in the rain

But everyone around you can see it

And no matter how real it is you never believe it

Even when their body is lying in the casket

And you stare at their grave every time that you pass it

It's never enough to prove that they're gone

Because in your heart and mind they still go on

You expect them to call and ask how you've been

But when they don't you remember that it's the end

And as each and every day passes by you think of it less

And every day it feels like less of a mess

But when you're alone it's still a punch in the gut

Because all the time in the world was never enough

In loving memory of a dear friend.

Rest In Peace,

Jason Lopez

Night Writing

I'm laying in my bed feeling like I'm on fire

Because for some reason I write a little better when I'm tired

And if I said I didn't like it, you could say I'm a liar

Because I love it when my head is spinning around like a tire

So I'll lay here and think and type a note in my phone

And I'll write about the days and nights I'm alone

About all the times I've been left at home

Because I was still asleep when my family was gone

Nobody woke me but the late alarm

But regret is just a word that's always far from my tongue

I've got no remorse for the work that I've done

So if I don't answer when you text you better leave me alone

Because I'm probably busy working on another song

And I'm trying to finish up before the night is gone

So I can try and get to sleep before the early dawn

On Edge

I don't need to lift just to keep my weapons sharp

Because my mind is at the ready and it's powered by my heart

Try to test my wit and I'll tear you all apart

Because I am on the edge and I'm rolling like an R

So don't push me, I'll do it myself

I'm not afraid to jump into the depths of Hell

Using my name as a battle cry I'll fight the world alone

Richard Jennings to the rescue, now you better run along

I've got a take no shit kind of attitude and a mouth that likes to move

My body's like some dynamite with a heart that hates to lose

On the edge between reality and insanity

It's a calamity and God damn it we

Don't know what to do

Unsure of which side to choose

So we stand in the middle on the blade

Until our halves slip into seperate graves

One for reality, the person we could really see

The other for insanity, the person we would choose to be

The differences may appear to be small

But the list is over a mile long

But with a gap that's spread so wide it spans a life

How could the desicion be made in the space on the edge of a knife?

Smoke Signals

You need to remember today, that his memories are
burning away, like the cigarettes that he's using, to remind
himself that he's still a human, being, as he searches the
smoke for some sign of a deeper meaning, because he's not
sure yet, but he'll surely never forget, how it feels to be in
love with you.

Out of Sight (Disappear)

You're right behind me all the time,
Just out of sight, but never out of mind,
And I can feel you when you're near,
but every time, I turn around, you disappear.
I never have to wonder if it's really true
I always know that it's really you
But when I turn around and you're not there
The sadness takes over, I can't hug the air

So in the poetic way that I speak
I beg you to be the prison, the shelter of the meek
My heart is strong but give credit where due
I'm only as good as I am because of you
So next time you're behind me
I beg that you don't blind me
Always out of sight, but never mind me
Always on my mind, but never remind me
I always feel you when you're near
So when I turn around, don't disappear

Owl

The Owls have always been my favorite animal at the zoo

And I see them every time I think of you

The understanding in their eyes, the fact that they know
what's wrong

The pain of being stuck where they don't belong

The Owls can fly, so they belong in the skies

But they're stuck in a cage, a prison of lies

Home is where the heart is, but they're not allowed to go

And if they're far from love, how can they call a cage home?

The answer is that they can't, and they have to suffer

They look up at the skies wishing to fly with their lovers

The only thing stopping them is the cage of impossibilities

Held by the ones who claim responsibility

The ones who claim to take care of the Owl

But it's a lie, the treatment is borderline foul

The Owl wishes it could fly

High into the skies

But deep inside its eyes

Is the understanding why

So the Owl sits, ever so patient

Receiving and giving looks that are ever so blatant

Biding time the Owl painfully waits

Until the perfect moment when they open the gates

The Owl takes flight, the keeper yells profanities

The wind on its face, its captor's calamity

The Owl has made it, finally free

On its way home, flying to me

So go home little Owl, follow your heart

To the place you knew you belonged from the start

Kill the Pain

O.D. on some pain pills

Hope they kill the way the pain feels

Because this shit is too real

The emotions and I can't deal

All the anger inside

And I'm a little terrified

That I might start losing my mind

Black out and go blind

And do something I might come to regret

To try and erase the things I want to forget

But if I let it go I might never get it back

So I'll just pop all the pills I have or better yet

Drown my sorrows in a bottle of Jack

Let the world know I won't be making it back

I hope it makes up for the courage I lack

When the bottle is empty and the world is turning black

Part of Me

Baby we're bringing heaven down

To where we are on the ground

I'm always happy when you're around

And you make it hard for me to frown

It's like hot chocolate on a cold night

Laying down by the fire light

And oh you're such a beautiful sight

And yeah you make me feel alright

It's the feeling I get when I see your face

It's the nerves I start to feel when my heart begins to race

It's the sound of your voice in every single thing you say

And the love in the sound when you're saying my name

You're the wonder of the world inside of my head

If I had to live without you I'd be better off dead

You're the thoughts on my mind when I'm laying in bed

And when you talk about me I still turn a shade of red

Baby you're the one I want
Baby you're the one I need
Baby you're in all my thoughts
Baby you're the blood I bleed
Baby you're a part of me

Sunrise Champion

Who needs to put their best foot forward
My horse has got his left hoof toward
The goal that I've been working for
We may be stuck standing over there
The wind's still blowing through my hair
Even though I'm going nowhere
It makes me feel empowered when my sword is raised
And the sun rises behind me like the sky is ablaze
If you could see it you would be amazed
You should really come and see if it's that true
Could the beauty of the world physically smack you?

Sinner's Angel

Maybe you'll let me hold your hand, and take you for a
walk. Maybe on that walk, we can stop and try to talk.
Maybe we can talk about the words we never spoke. Maybe
we can try and speak between the smoke. The space
between us is a battle ground and there will be no winner.
It's hard to find the common ground between the sin and
sinner. We need to try and clear the air before I can commit
you. I need you more than the other ones that cheated and
tried to hit you. I want you to know that I do really miss

you. And given the chance, I would still try and kiss you. But the space between us burns, it's hotter than a fire. How can we grow closer as a lie and a liar? Love was my existence, I could only spell "we." But with all the words you say, there are three that you keep. Maybe we can walk and talk, and sort all of this out. But I'm a sinner you're my angel, and you can't use your mouth. You can't tell me that you miss me, and after all this time you love me still. I can only hope to catch a glimpse of love, using your eyes as a window sill. I can try to see inside you, as I did so long ago. But I can't if you won't let me, so you've got to let me know.

Poets

These days everyone's a poet

Dripping creativity and not afraid to show it

Rhyming words in the same scheme until they think they know it

Waiting for a chance to blow because they know they'll never blow it

But when no one is the same and everbody's different

Just know that we are all the same in our difference

It's a shame we waste so much time fighting conformity

When we should be learning to act more formally

That would be a bore when the norm is to conform to the enormity

The mass of nonconforming abnormity

It needs an invasion of new culture as badly as Normandy

And what better crowd than a bunch of people who have never even heard of me?

Everyone's a poet but nobody writes poems

They can play with words but don't play games in their homes

They can structure schemes but don't know their own pattern of bones

And it's hard to talk to them when their poems are their phones

They weave and spin an intricate lie

They bleed and they spill secrets that die

They couldn't slow down and they have no clue why

Their poems aren't finished they're a finishing sigh

When no one is the same and everybody's different

Just know that we are all the same in our difference

When everyone's a true poet there are truly none

Because when everyone's a true poet the true poets are gone

Recognition

He out lasts every obstacle like a rock, it amazes

Every challenge that he faces on a day to day basis

It's taught him to see through all the smiling faces

To find that the recognition's in all the wrong places

He works harder than anyone he's ever known

At work more often than anytime he's ever home

He suffers a struggle that he knows can be never shown

And the indignity is that of a good man left alone

He's got friends who live like he knows he should

And he constantly thinks that one day he would

When he has everything he needs and he finally could

But it's in the hands of others and that much he understood

But they never noticed his work ethic

They never saw his shine

And when the time for recognition comes you guessed it

He's the unsung hero at the back of the line

Behind the scenes and working on the strings

With no reciprocation of material things

All he ever wanted was the freedom of wings

But they gave him wings of iron so he learned instead to sing

He sung to build his lungs some strength, he would need it in the air

His eyes were never on the ground, he wouldn't be down there

He continued to do what he always did and outworked everyone near

Until he built the strength to flap his wings and feel the wind in his air

So don't hold back the unsung hero, help him as he goes

His potential can be limitless if you help him as he grows

He can soar across the sky giving life to a murder of crows

The potential of the unsung hero is the recognition nobody shows

Roll Harder

I haven't practiced in a while

And it may be detrimental to my style

But if there's one thing I know

It's that I've still got the flow

And it's only getting bigger so

You better watch it as it grows

I listen to Biggie and Pac

DMX and Nas

So if you want to scrap

You better put up the paws

I got the game on lock

Like I'm pressin on pause

And I'm down to roll deep

Brawling just because

So don't push because I push back

I'll give you a lyrical heart attack

Catch my crew in the black on black

When they put it down I'm picking up the slack

Quicker than slick I'm faster than Flash

Stay out of my lane or you're getting passed

Focus on the future and making it last

I don't really care about the past

I'm rolling hard and going farther

You go hard but I'm going harder

You can't keep up don't even bother

I'll eat you up like Jeffrey Dahmer

Royal Love

Here ye, here ye, listen to me.

This is the story of the King and the Queen.

Her love was a fire and his soul gasoline.

She fueled his desires and ignited his dreams.

No good for each other but they would never leave.

One day they got too close for comfort.

They couldn't bear to be apart from each other.

So they reached out and they touched one another.

The friction and heat of love that couldn't be bothered.

They created a fire that couldn't be smothered.

Together they thought they could master fate.

But they never knew it could be too late.

So plan they did for their escape.

They met at midnight by the gates.

But the enemy knew and set the bait.

The King alone, now stranded outside.

The Queen he loved had left him and lied.

The enemy had her on their side.

On this day The King's heart died.

But he fought on to survive the night.

The Eye

Feel the wind blow through your hair

Can you tell the storm is there?

A refreshing breeze and tumbling leaves

Lulls you into a sense of ease

You take satisfaction in surviving the first

But you still have yet to face the worst

But you've been through worse before

So stare into the eye of the storm

Sake of a Song

You see I planned to sleep, and then came dawn. What would you do for the sake of a song? Stay up late and masturbate? Find a new way to procrastinate? Headphones on and the music up. Repeating the beat until it's all used up? Tap tap tap go the keys on the board. Your head on the desk when you get bored. Sitting still hours at a time. Just trying to write another line. When you say you've had enough, the page is there to call your bluff. But there's nothing left to write about. All your ideas are all played out. Tomorrow morning you'll learn a lesson. You'll know the answer to the question.

What would you do for the sake of a song?

Write all night cause it takes so long?

Would you stay up until the dawn?

What would you do for the sake of a song?

Shit Happens

Young kid going in thinking he's going to kill it
Putting it all forward hoping you're going to feel it
So he can get off the streets and stop stealing
Because his cards don't make a hand and the dealer has
stopped dealing
Lucky for him he's good enough to leave your mind reeling
And soon enough he'll be able to reach the ceiling
Which is good
I hope he gets what he deserves
Because the kid has got a message and he's got to be heard
And if no one listens when he talks then he'll put it in a
verse
And people are more sympathetic when perspective's in the
third
So he'll tell you a story you'll wish you never heard
And he'll teach you things about him that you'll wish you
never learned
Every memory never faded
Every bridge he never burned
And how he learned the lesson
Penny saved, penny earned

Some people aren't born to make it
Some people have to get up and take it
It's a cruel world to grow up in
But life moves on, and shit happens

So the other day, I heard the story of a kid
A boy who decided it wasn't enough just to exist
So he picked himself up and he decided to live
Went out in the world and gave it all he could give
Eating out of plastic ware without any lids
No money for plates in the apartment he lived
He barely scraped by enough to pay the rent
Grateful for the fact that they let him move in
But the part of the story that made me spin
I thought it was sad but that was just the beginning
The kid set out to make it and make it he did
Singing songs and rapping in sold out gigs
Looking back at himself and the life that he lived
Glad that he decided to do more than exist

Some people aren't born to make it
Some people have to get up and take it
It's a cruel world to grow up in
But life moves on, and shit happens

Shout Out to My Ex

Shout out to my ex who stole my heart from my chest

Treated me like the rest when she knew I was the best

Images spinning in my eyes of her in a dress

I was stressed, needed rest, feelin down, wishin' death

She cut me open, left me bleedin from my heart and my head

But I'm too damn strong to lay down and play dead

So don't hold your breath 'cause it ain't over yet

Im surviving every time so get to placing your bets

She couldn't kill me and I'm only growing stronger

From the moment that she said she didn't love me any longer

Said I was like family a cousin or a brother

Completely ignoring the fact that I was her lover

But I haven't gone away and I'm consistently persistent

I'm just waiting for the day that she would sit down and listen

Bump the stereo loud and hear a beautiful song

Hear my voice say her name and wonder what's going on

What is he saying about be man? What's the deal?

Then I say a word to let her know that it's real

She was my dream and now I'm giving her nightmares

Hit me below the belt and now it's too late to fight fair

This ain't a shout out it's a mother fuckin' battle cry

Let you walk on me? Listen up 'cause I'd rather die

No longer will you get to push me around

I've been laid out and kicked when I was down

When you're feeling lonely and you get to missing this

I want you to think about me and your viciousness

How you let me go without a heart or a hope

Hangin' off a cliff you tied a noose in the rope

When it came time to do it or let it die

You tied me to a horse and told them to let it ride

But to your surprise, I made it out alive

And now I'm here making you wish that I had died

Sure I was a joke, and you hit me with the punch line

But now I've got a flow serving up like a lunch line

Situations and Circumstances

Situations, circumstances, yeah we never had a chance when, you were the first girl I danced with, I wonder what really happened, to the girl I fell in love with.

Steel myself and dig in deeper, love just got a whole lot cheaper, you will never have to leave her, and you won't be the deceiver, because that bitch left you first.

Which is okay because now I know, there is always a tomorrow, we hang out with different people, and when invited to try and go, anywhere she never shows, which is cool by me.

I'm not going to try and justify a word said by a cold hearted bitch. I'm not going to sit here and think of all the dreams I should've never wished. Wasted time was good while it lasted, and I wish that was true, but I can't help laughing. Because quite frankly it kind of sucked. Smiling seldom, hurting often, putting nails into the coffin, of this cold, dead, love.

Some would say we shouldn't blame ourselves because it wasn't our fault. But who can we honestly blame if not? And I'm not here to give a lecture, I'm just thinking of the bigger picture. Why did we sit here and let it go to waste? Was there even any reason, or did you decide one season, that you got tired of the taste?

And don't get me wrong, I'm not nearly done, I'm just trying to put the pieces in the puzzle. Because for us to be, you need to see, the voice of love just can't be muzzled. I can't hold my tongue because you say so. I refuse. You can't come back just because you're lonely, because I can't tell if you truly want me. I won't be used. You can't make me wait any longer than is fair, and then just leave me hanging in the air. I'm not having it. I've sacrificed for you both life and limb, and catered to your every whim. It's a load of shit. So this is my ultimatum. A decree, if you will. That no more love shall be lost, and no more blood shall be spilled. And I know that I just went off, and I should probably try and chill, but I just thought that you should know, if you show me I should leave, I will.

Snack Breaks

She loved swimming. She spent her time out on the lakes. She only ate certain foods when she took her breaks. But when she broke her diet, there was one food she would always make. It was little bits of pretzels sprinkled on top of a batch of cupcakes.

When she baked them, her cabin would fill with the smell. When people came to visit her they could always tell. The vanilla extract in the air was swell. She knew when they were done by the sound of a bell.

Finally gathered, her friends all wait for a taste. Hungry and tired, fresh from a race. Soon enough the sound of crunching fills the space. Her pretzel cupcakes put smiles on everybody's face.

Tell me, which high is the realest?

We had it all, and we had it all figured out.

The world at our feet and no reason to doubt.

Backs against the wall and ready to shout,

Because we knew what life was about.

But when you walked away you took the whole plan with you.

I followed along until I heard that a grown man hit you.

You broke up with him and I thought I had a chance,

But you kept on running while I was becoming a man.

And now that I know better I'm no longer with it.

Because I was never the type to hit it and quit it.

I need a girl who can appreciate what I'm worth,

And love me for me without leaving me in the dirt.

So good luck, I hope you have a nice life.

I mean that sincerely, I hope you get your life right.

And when you do, there'll be good things to see.

But don't wait up, because they won't include me.

I'm done, gone, and I'm not looking back.

I'm building a future and that won't start with the past.

Squiggle Attraction

I suppose I should say something.
Even if it turns out to be nothing.
But even nothing is something even if it's only the sound of
me breathing heavy. And even that's poetic I guess. I would
say something great if you'd let me, but you're making me
nervous and my head is a mess. I can't think straight. That's
always been a problem for me as far back as I can
remember. I've always been thinking in squiggles, and
circles, and squares, and dodecagons. But not straight lines.
No, never. They never end and go for as long as I can
remember and that's been a problem for me because for as
long as I can remember that's been the only thing linear
about my thoughts. It's the fact that they're not. Dreams,
nightmares, fantasies, and hopes all burning in a circular
melting pot. Stirred up by a squiggular spoon held by a
square chanting in a dodecagon drawn in sidewalk chalk
under the moon. And I've thoroughly creeped myself out.
Because who thinks of things like this? Nobody normal I
assure you. I would be scared to speak like this if I didn't
entirely adore you. And I do mean all of you. Not any
particular one. Well, maybe one or two of you more than
the others. But I'm still trying to decide on my reasons not
to. Maybe you've got herpes. Or maybe you're too much
like my mother. Either way I'm justifying ignorance
because no matter how much I adore you I can't think
straight enough to talk so I can only hope to ignore you.
And maybe you'll see that for the sign that it is and you'll
come say something to me. Or maybe you won't and I'll
just stay here and sit tight in my circular tragedy. Either

way I won't say a word at all. I won't even scream as I hit
the floor because I'll be too busy hoping you'll catch me as
I fall. So that's why the entire time that I've been up here, I
haven't said a single word. Later on I won't know what
poem you're referring to because I don't know what it is
you think you've heard. But I can tell you that it wasn't me.
I can't think straight enough to talk. What you heard was
how nervous I would be, if you would hold my hand and go
for a walk.

What Next

That cool slow breeze on those hot summer nights
The way your hair shines with the glow of moonlight
Why don't you step back down to my level a moment
Your hand is looking soft and I just want to hold it
Your eyes reflect the fire that we're both sitting next to
I get nervous and ask myself what would the best do?
This girl is the one I want to give this world and the rest to
She's the beat that makes the heart in my chest move
I can't help but wonder who makes the next move?
I want to kiss you on the lips just to test you

Steel and Stone

She says I'm a dream but I assure you I'm still real, but I can't give a crap because my balls are made of steel. I stay getting mine, it's like I made a deal, and paper chasers tripping like I dropped banana peels. I'm just trying to put in time. Just trying to get what's mine. Writing line for line, until the day I'm dying, just to get this off my mind. I've gotten cold. Or so I've been told. And there's not a thing I own, that I wouldn't have sold, just to make this house a home. But I couldn't give a shit if I tried, the lines are all busy and the operator's fired. There ain't no way to reach me, and no one could ever teach me, so don't go and try to preach to me, about how you think we should be, because I'm not listening, and I'm going to keep on doing me, and you know I'll stay living free. So bug about it. Give a shit. Turn the fan on and watch it hit. Now clean it up. Yeah I'm cold. Balls of steel and a heart of stone.

Yeah, I got a call from this girl the other day. She said she just wanted to talk and say hey. But we all know how that story ends. It's the same with all my ex-girlfriends. She said I'm cold but that she's still in love with me. So I turned her down and gave her freezer burn of the third degree. It's only right after what she put me through. Took my heart, crushed it, and broke it right in two. And she has the nerve to ask me why I'm cold. Because she turned me into solid Steel and Stone. So now I stick to what I know, and that's how to treat these hoes, when they act up. And everybody

knows, that when it comes to blows, I just don't give a fuck.
So holler when you see me. Let me know what's up. And if
you call me family then you better back it up. Because I'm
tired of these lames. They keep on playing games.
Claiming that they know me but they don't know my
middle name. So I'm done, it won't be tolerated. People
want the world from me ever since I graduated. But no.
You can go get your own. Because you can't share
blood with a man of Steel and Stone.

The Sick Boy

There's a place in a town in a state in a nation, where
there's a boy at a desk in a room who needs some
medication. He's sick and it's not your typical disease. Only
smoke comes out when he tries to breathe. Everything he's
seen once drawn up in beauty, now drowned out in the call
of his duty. The duty to his family, duty to himself. The call
of duty that calls him to his own private hell. He can't get
out, no he can't find the door. Nobody understands, he
doesn't want to be here anymore. He's got cabin fever and a
need to know, who he is and how far he can go. What he's
willing to do and what he's willing to lose, and when he
gets the chance, what he's willing to choose.

Suicide Notes and Love Letters

"Sometimes I just want to be forgotten about"

Don't ever let me hear you put those words in your mouth

That's a lie and you know it, now spit it out!

You just want to know what life and love are about

Tired of wolf whistles and "hey girl" shouts

You just want someone to love a side aside from the out

So before you lose yourself in the weather

I just want to let you know it gets better

I tried to tell her to listen to some words

Unfortunately they could never be heard

Because she decided she wanted to end it all

Pulled the trigger one night in a bathroom stall

I just wanted to say that I loved her

Held her high with only heaven above her

And now I know that all that glitters isn't gold

And the gleam in her eyes were just the scars on her soul

The Fall

The ones that say they'll never fall, always drop like rocks. That's what happens when they're on the edge, and the only way is off. Welcome to the Edge Hotel, with a smile we welcome all. You should really see the roof, just try your hardest not to fall. But remember you won't be alone, there'll always be a friendly voice. You may not even want to jump, you may not even have the choice. I'll see you up there again real soon, way up at the top. And then I'll see you down here again, this won't be the last time you drop. The ones that say they'll never fall, always drop like rocks. That's what happens when they're on the edge, and the only way is off. You can try to say it didn't happen, try to claim you never fell. But I see every bump and bruise, every sign there is to tell. I see all that come and go, and all that come and go again. And I've witnessed a thousand times, the rise and fall of you my friend. So you can try to play it cool, act like it didn't happen. But it's all too obvious, that the hard ground isn't padded. But say what you want, do what you will. I've been through the fall, I know it's a thrill. It's a vicious cycle, an addictive pain. But for some reason, you all still fall like rain. My shift is almost over, I'll see you up there soon. I think this time, I might jump to reach the moon. But no matter what, I always know. I won't fly, I'll fall like snow. The ones that say they'll never fall, always drop like rocks. That's what happens when they're on the edge, and the only way is off.

The Government

The government is for the people by the people of the
people, but only seems to be missing the people. It's like a
church without a steeple, a door without a peephole, it's
hollow, and meaningless, and defeats the purpose. It's
nothing but delegation, deliberation, deliberate allegation,
defamation, and the cause of inflation in the nation. More
money for the army than the relief, the people are in a state
of disbelief. State of the union? Ha! It's the state of the
sheep. Herded to the cliff and ready to leap. Don't leap and
at a word there'll be a push. And then everybody will be in
a rush, and nobody will stop to think it's too much. So
whatever happened to the people being in the government
for the people by the people of the people that's missing the
people?

The Man(iac) Inside

There's something building inside of me. A murderous rage.

The desire to spill the blood and spread it across the page.

A story told by words written in murder and ink.

A song so greusome you have to stop and think.

Is he for real? Could this be true?

Afraid because it could be you.

The victim in the papers and on tv.

The killer who's eyes are as cold as can be.

Be victim for pleasure or the killer for thrill.

The world is full of maniacs just dying to kill.

Cannibals, Animals, MONSTERS, and MEN!

When the rush wears off YOU DO IT AGAIN.

But no. Not you. Not a chance. NEVER.

You're a GOOD person. You've been that way forever.

But given a push, we'll see how far you can fall.

Soon enough you'll find out there's a maniac inside of us all.

The Victim

I'm walking home in the rain from a long day at work

Reflecting on the pain I felt in your smirk

When I stumbled onto a murder scene I could tell was gruesome

A witness told me the victim was one of a twosome

And the other had been the killer

That the lover had been the killer

The victim had shown up the day after a fight

They had a disagreement to end an otherwise wonderful night

He had made an attempt to make an ammend

But it brought him to an early end

My kingdom for a horse bought a horse for the land

But even a horse couldn't save him from her hand

She threw him down the stairs to the ground under the nook

Then chased him down screaming and ground his neck under her foot

She went upstairs leaving him there on the ground for all to see

A heartbroken mess to sadden a person like me

The helpless victim in too bad of a shape to be outlined in chalk

The white rose that lay smashed at my feet on the sidewalk

Tick Back

Every good day is stained with black, and when the clock ticks, it won't, tick, back. Every second lost is a wasted breath, edging closer to the edge of death. Every thought not put to words, the silence of a little bird. Every feeling not expressed, someone leaves with the pain of regret. Every hello that was never waved, could have been a bridge but was never paved. Every goodbye that was never said, was never the last before forever bed. The truth that goes unknown, the cover never blown. The fact that you can't escape the fact, that the past is never coming back. Every good day is stained with black, and when the clock ticks, it won't, tick, back.

True Meanings

Listen to the keys tapping away as I type. Listen to the unfolding story of my life. See the concentration behind my brown eyes. See the adulation that I have for my lies. Falsities, sugar coated truths. More misunderstood than "these two youths." Things that you think are what I really meant to say. But the sting in the words has been taken away. What I want you to hear would leave you with a burn. That way you won't forget the lesson you learn. But I'm not that good at letting bridges crumble. I keep on looking back and it keeps on making me stumble. So I change some things here and there. I cloud the meaning in smoke to clear the air. You can try to make the messages out if you dare it. They may not be about you, but if it fits then wear it.But like I said, I add and take and leave things out. You can guess and think bu you'll always have doubt. You'll never know the true message I want to send. I'll take my secrets with me until the end. But that doesn't mean I'll take them to grave. Only until they don't need to be saved.

What Can I Do?

This blank page on my screen is taunting me. This poem won't write itself.

The sound of her voice in my head is haunting me. It's telling me I might need some help.

But who can I ask about a dying love? One that's given up on me?

And what can I take for a broken heart? One that's not meant to be?

What can I do to ease the pain? The remorse of her regret?

What can I use to escape her name? To help me try and forget?

How can she give up on us? When she knows I never have?

Why do I continue to push? And give it all I can?

My love is a fire and it's out of control. But I could never put it out.

Maybe while raging it'll warm her soul. And she'll light all shadows of doubt.

Maybe while burning it will light her path. Maybe she'll find the road.

Maybe she'll be able to do the math. Maybe she'll finally know.

Maybe she'll see that there's more to see. Because there always is.

Maybe she'll see there's more to me. More than just a kid.

I need her to know that I'm grown and wise. Reliable and honest too.

I need her to know the truth in the words. When I tell her "I love you."

When Life Gets Hard

It's hard to see when the lights are off and the walls are black

It's hard to breathe when there's no windows and the door has no crack

It's hard to feel scared when the walls are padded and soft

It's hard to keep your feet on the ground when your head is aloft

It's hard to focus on sanity when the drugs keep you blurred

It's hard to pray to God when even the words in your thoughts are slurred

It's even harder still just to sit still when you're on so many pills

It's harder than that just to recap who you are and where you're at

It's a problem when you can't remember the name of your wife

It's impossible to write when you can't recall the story of your own life

But it's easy to let it all go to Hell

It's easy to forget the stories you can't tell

It's easier to accept that you might die in this room

It's harder to live than meet your doom

It's easy to lay down and let time pass you by

It's easy to give up and wish to die

It's easier to surrender than it is to fight

It's harder to do but I always choose the light

It's hard to make the desicions nobody else can

It's hard to take on the responsibilities of a man

It's easy to go with the flow and let things happen

It's hard to live and love, but I love to live a challenge

Where I'm From

Let me tell you about the town I was raised in

The place I've lived and I've played in

Newburgh, New York where I went to school

My city's got a rep but the people in it do too

My city's been known for violence and drugs

Alchohal and blood in equal parts stain the rugs

But I've never been worried about that either way

Because it's not completely as bad as people say

From the children at the park in Little League

To the taco truck parked on the side of the street

There's little things to love every where you turn

And if you want to, it's never too late to learn

So make your comments, and I'll let it slide

Because people from my city say it with pride

You've heard a few things, you're not the only one

We've never been afraid to be where we're from

It doesn't phase us because we love this place

It made us who we are and for that we give thanks

Some may leave but they're quickly replaced

There's no shortage of people to join our ranks

And we can't be so bad when they keep on coming

Because if we were they would all end up running

Your city is your home no matter where you're from, so don't judge me based on my city alone.

Who I Would Save

If I had a time machine and a list of names

Followed by reasons of people to save

I would throw the list right down the drain

I'm changing history in my own way

First off I would start with my dad

That's common sense, and nobody could be mad

There were things I could use some advice on

And my dad has never led me wrong

Second off I'd keep hitler from killing himself

I'd make sure he suffered his own personal Hell

Because you don't do what he did without paying a price

Being a massive dick on a global scale is not alright

Next I would save Biggie and Tupac

I would force them to reconcile and come save hip-hop

They would be friends again and take back the game

From that point on things would never be the same

Lyrics would be deeper and words would be played with

I would gladly take the rap game we have now and trade it

Next I would save John F. Kennedy and Abraham Lincoln

Honestly, what were those assassins thinking?

They were possibly the two greatest leaders America's ever had

They died years ago and it still makes people sad

These are the people I would save, if I wasn't time's slave

Why Does This Happen

Why? Why after all this time, does your memory still haunt me?

Always in the back of my mind, why do you still have the power to taunt me?

You were the one who walked away when I prayed you would stay and you had nothing to say for yourself or why you were acting this way. I was the one who suffered the indignity when you took a piece after I let you into me and just to get it back I took to the holy trinity. They took their time with the reparation, and no matter the preparation I wasn't prepared for the devastation you left in the wake of the abomination you called our love. But no matter how strong I thought it was, to you it was never enough. I bet it all and you called my bluff, so when I lost you cashed out with everything I had. At first I was sad, and then I got mad, but I finally got over it and somehow I was glad. But now I realize I was mistaken. I'm still missing the piece that you've taken. Unable to feel, the remnants of my heart are misshapen. Somehow I still secretly hope that you want me. And after all this time your memory still has the power to haunt me. Always in the back of my mind it continuously taunts me.

Work Harder

If you want to succeed you'll work until 6am and fall asleep
with the tape recorder still rolling

And then you wake up 3 hours later talking in your sleep
and you're still going

That's the kind of life you live if you want to do more than
just exist

And that's the kind of work you put in to be more than just
a name on a list

And if you're lucky you get to be the list maker

But if you're not than you're just a sick waiter

Pushing carts full of dishes to be cleaned and reused

While you'd rather be downtown at the cigar bar singing
the blues

But you've got bills to pay and it's way too risky

But as a waiter when's the last time you got frisky?

You've witnessed people put in work and it seemed to get
them pretty far

Now imagine what your life would be like if you worked
twice as hard

Humble Narcissism

One more poem to finish this book and it won't be an apology. Because my life is commonly a comedy when people are constantly gossipy. But I'm an oddity honestly, I'm more like a modesty homily. You told a prophecy sloppily and summoned the prodigy. You thought it was you, but you unlocked the God in me, you wannabe. I'm an anomaly, predicted by astronomy to ruin the autonomy of your dishonesty with ferocity. Your hypocrisy is imposibly a monstrosity. You lie constantly and it's monotony in quantity, but I don't expect an apology or equality. It's already gotten me too bent on writing the biography of your mediocrity to sit here solemnly.

The End

I hope you enjoyed reading this as much as I enjoyed writing it.

As always, thank you for reading.

Sincerely,

Richard Jennings

www.ingramcontent.com/pod-product-compliance
Lightning Source LLC
Chambersburg PA
CBHW061957040426

42447CB00010B/1795